W9-AVK-368

CENTER YOUR LIFE ON

Jesus

A 40-DAY DEVOTIONAL

Mikal Keefer

Jesus-Centered Devotions

Center Your Life on *Jesus*
A 40-Day Devotional

Copyright © 2016 Group Publishing, Inc.

group.com

Inspired by *The Jesus-Centered Life* by Rick Lawrence. All rights reserved.
No part of this book may be reproduced in any manner whatsoever without
prior written permission from the publisher, except in the case of brief
quotations embodied in critical articles and reviews. For information, visit
group.com/permissions.

Scripture quotations marked CEB are taken from the Common English
Bible®, CEB®. Copyright © 2010, 2011 by Common English Bible™. Used by
permission. All rights reserved worldwide.

Scripture quotations marked CEV are from the Contemporary English Version.
Copyright © 1991, 1992, 1995 by American Bible Society. Used by permission.

Scripture quotations marked GNT are from the Good News Translation ©
1994 published by the Bible Societies/HarperCollins Publishers Ltd UK,
Good News Bible © American Bible Society 1966, 1971, 1976, 1992. Used
with permission.

Scripture quotations marked GW are from *God's Word*, a copyrighted work
of God's Word to the Nations. Quotations are used by permission. Copyright
1995 by God's Word to the Nations. All rights reserved.

Scripture quotations marked NASB are taken from the New American Standard
Bible®. Copyright © 1960, 1962, 1963, 1968, 1971, 1972, 1973,1975, 1977,
1995 by The Lockman Foundation. Used by permission. (www.Lockman.org)

Scripture quotations marked NIV are taken from THE HOLY BIBLE, NEW
INTERNATIONAL VERSION®, NIV®. Copyright © 1973, 1978, 1984, 2011 by
Biblica, Inc.® Used by permission. All rights reserved worldwide.

Scripture quotations marked NLT are taken from the *Holy Bible*, New Living
Translation, copyright © 1996, 2004, 2015 by Tyndale House Foundation.
Used by permission of Tyndale House Publishers, Inc., Carol Stream, Illinois
60188. All rights reserved.

Scripture quotations marked TLB are from The Living Bible copyright © 1971
by Tyndale House Foundation. Used by permission of Tyndale House Publishers
Inc., Carol Stream, Illinois 60188. All rights reserved. The Living Bible, TLB, and
The Living Bible logo are registered trademarks of Tyndale House Publishers.

ISBN 978-1-4707-4274-4

10 9 8 7 6 5 4 3 2 1   25 24 23 22 21 20 19 18 17 16

Printed in the United States of America.

DURING HIS LIFE ON EARTH, JESUS ASKED LOTS OF QUESTIONS.

That was true then...and it's true now.

The Gospels are packed with Jesus' questions.

Questions that prompted conversations. Raised issues. Opened eyes to flashes of discovery and insight.

And Jesus' questions tended to follow people home, to roll around in their minds, to insist on answers.

So...here are 40 opportunities to answer them.

You'll respond to questions Jesus posed to people around him. And as you do, you'll invite Jesus into conversations about what his questions reveal about him...and what your answers reveal about you.

So come hear his voice.

Feel his presence.

And experience time with Jesus that refreshes your spirit, sparks fresh insight, and draws the two of you closer together.

Then he got into the boat and his disciples followed him. Suddenly a furious storm came up on the lake, so that the waves swept over the boat.

But Jesus was sleeping.

The disciples went and woke him, saying, 'Lord, save us! We're going to drown!'

He replied, 'You of little faith, why are you so afraid?' Then he got up and rebuked the winds and the waves, and it was completely calm.

—Matthew 8:23-26, NIV

CENTER YOUR LIFE ON JESUS

WHY ARE YOU SO AFRAID ?

Jesus' disciples never seem to have accused him of asking a stupid question.

But if it ever did happen, it happened here.

Late in the day, a sudden squall caught Jesus and his followers in open water on the Sea of Galilee.

The wind rose, the sky darkened, rain slashed the disciples' faces. And as calm water roiled into white-capped waves, the disciples knew: This is where they'd die.

Water cascaded over the hull of the wooden boat, swamping the already-floundering vessel.

And then the full fury of the storm crashed in on them.

Shaken awake, Jesus looked into the faces of his terrified disciples and shouted over the screaming gale: "Why are you so afraid?"

Why were they *afraid*? *Afraid*? Wasn't it *obvious*?

The disciples stared at one another, thinking, *Even a carpenter's kid should see what's happening here.*

But they'd misunderstood the question.

Jesus was really asking, "Why are you so afraid...*when I'm with you*?"

Fair question.

They'd gotten to know Jesus. Heard him teach. Seen him perform miracles.

Sort of like you.

You've gotten to know Jesus. Heard him teach. Perhaps seen his power shine in your life and the lives of people you know.

So why are you afraid? Of loss. Death. Living a life of Jesus-centered abandon?

Given that Jesus is with you... why are you so afraid?

And what might set you free from your fear?

AS YOU SPOKE WITH JESUS,
WHAT DID YOU DISCOVER ABOUT HIM?

Worry about being able to take
care of myself financially
worry about having a close
fun relationship w/my children
+ grandchildren

AS JESUS SPOKE WITH YOU, WHAT DID HE HELP YOU DISCOVER ABOUT YOURSELF?

he loves me, he knows my
fears & will be w/me
I do not need to be afraid
because he will shower
me w/love & kindness

And why worry about a
speck in the eye of a
brother when you have a board
in your own?

—Matthew 7:3, TLB

WHY WORRY ABOUT A SPECK IN THE EYE OF A BROTHER ?

Think Jesus never cracked a joke?

Think again.

A crowd had gathered to hear Jesus teach, so he did what teachers of his time always did: He sat down as his students stood, fanning out around him.

He talked with them about who they were, about anger, adultery, and divorce. He touched on prayer and money, and then came the crowd pleaser.

Then came the joke.

A guy with a board in his eye trying to help remove the speck from a friend's eye?

Hilarious.

Picture everyone chuckling, laughter rippling as people elbowed each other and pointed to Jesus. *Good one. Reminds of me Joanna back home.*

And then Jesus paused, letting the truth sink in: It wasn't Joanna he had in mind.

It was the people standing in front of him on that rocky hillside.

It was them…and us.

Perhaps even you.

Why *do* we judge others so harshly? Why *are* we so prone to ignore our own faults and focus on those of others?

What fuels our arrogance and sense of self-righteousness?

How do you answer Jesus' question?

WHY WORRY ABOUT A SPECK IN THE EYE OF A BROTHER ?

AS YOU SPOKE WITH JESUS, WHAT DID YOU DISCOVER ABOUT HIM?

AS JESUS SPOKE WITH YOU, WHAT DID HE HELP YOU DISCOVER ABOUT YOURSELF?

> So I tell you to stop worrying about what you will eat, drink, or wear. Isn't life more than food and the body more than clothes?
>
> Look at the birds. They don't plant, harvest, or gather the harvest into barns. Yet, your heavenly Father feeds them. Aren't you worth more than they?
>
> Can any of you add a single hour to your life by worrying?

—Matthew 6:25-27, GW

CENTER YOUR LIFE ON JESUS

CAN YOU ADD A SINGLE HOUR TO YOUR LIFE BY WORRYING (?)

When Jesus suggested living a worry-free life, he was talking to people who had a lot to worry about.

Most of Jesus' audience was illiterate, scraping by day-to-day with little hope for a softer, easier future. Poverty and disease ground them down, and violence at the hands of their Roman occupiers was commonplace.

A third of their children died in infancy, and a third of those who survived infancy were dead by the age of 6. The average life expectancy of the men listening to Jesus was just 29, making him, in his early 30s, something of an elder statesman.

But could worry lengthen the days of those listening to Jesus? ease their burdens? give them hope?

Jesus' question is one he lays at the doorstep of each of his followers…including you.

You, too, have your list of worries. Finances, health, relationships, an uncertain future, or unsettled past—they can all crowd into your thinking and commandeer your focus.

Where will the money come from? How can the healing happen?

What's next…and how can you prepare?

Jesus' question isn't meant to mock or scold—it's meant to guide you.

If worrying doesn't help, why does it nip so often at your heels?

And what might you do to be rid of it?

CAN YOU ADD A SINGLE HOUR TO YOUR LIFE BY WORRYING ?

AS YOU SPOKE WITH JESUS,
WHAT DID YOU DISCOVER ABOUT HIM?

_____

_____

_____

_____

_____

_____

_____

_____

_____

_____

CENTER YOUR LIFE ON JESUS

AS JESUS SPOKE WITH YOU, WHAT DID HE HELP YOU DISCOVER ABOUT YOURSELF?

So Peter went over the side of the boat and walked on the water toward Jesus.

But when he saw the strong wind and the waves, he was terrified and began to sink. 'Save me, Lord!' he shouted.

Jesus immediately reached out and grabbed him. 'You have so little faith,' Jesus said. 'Why did you doubt me?'

—Matthew 14:29-31, NLT

WHY DID YOU DOUBT ME (?)

Strange day for Peter.

He'd seen Jesus miraculously feed thousands (good day).

Then he'd struggled against storm-driven waves and contrary winds to sail across the Sea of Galilee (bad day).

Exhausted, sometime after 3:00 a.m., he'd spotted Jesus *walking on water* (amazing day) and gotten Jesus' okay to leap out of the boat and walk over to him.

At which point he promptly sank (worst day *ever*).

Jesus' response, as he hauled Peter up and out of danger: "You have so little faith. Why did you doubt me?"

Jesus never condemned those who came to him with honest doubts—not when he walked the earth, and not now. To Jesus, honest doubts are an entrance ramp to relationship, to a growing, vibrant faith.

Today, answer Jesus' question. What does cause you to doubt him or his love for you?

What are the questions you'd most like Jesus to answer? The concerns that don't seem safe to raise when you're with other people of faith?

Have a fearless conversation with Jesus.

Answer his question: Why do you doubt him?

Then listen for his response.

AS YOU SPOKE WITH JESUS, WHAT DID YOU DISCOVER ABOUT HIM?

AS JESUS SPOKE WITH YOU, WHAT DID HE HELP YOU DISCOVER ABOUT YOURSELF?

When Jesus came to the region of Caesarea Philippi, he asked his disciples, 'Who do people say the Son of Man is?'

They replied, 'Some say John the Baptist; others say Elijah; and still others, Jeremiah or one of the prophets.'

'But what about you?' he asked. 'Who do you say I am?'

—Matthew 16:13-15, NIV

WHO DO YOU SAY I AM ?

"Who do people say I am?"

Jesus didn't ask his disciples this question because he was insecure or unsure of himself. Jesus knew precisely who he was and what he was about.

He asked because then—as now—most people don't really know the answer.

The disciples quickly summed up what they'd heard.

Some people thought Jesus was like John the Baptist, pushing a program of national repentance. Others pegged him as a new Elijah, a miracle worker.

And still others considered Jesus a modern-day Jeremiah, God's spokesperson standing up to corrupt rulers and religious blowhards.

Jesus listened, nodded, and then pressed his question home.

"But you," he said, leaning in, "Who do *you* say I am?"

This wasn't just a question, it was *the* question, and then—as now—everything hinges on your answer.

It's tempting to underestimate Jesus. Yes, he worked miracles. Yes, he stood up to political and religious abuse. Yes, he pointed out the need for repentance.

That's true—but it's not the whole truth.

He was all of that, but he was more…much more.

Then and now.

Jesus' question is still *the* question—and it still hangs in the air, waiting for your answer.

Who do *you* say Jesus is?

And how does your answer shape your life?

AS YOU SPOKE WITH JESUS,
WHAT DID YOU DISCOVER ABOUT HIM?

CENTER YOUR LIFE ON JESUS

AS JESUS SPOKE WITH YOU, WHAT DID HE HELP YOU DISCOVER ABOUT YOURSELF?

> Knowing their thoughts, Jesus said,
> 'Why do you entertain evil
> thoughts in your hearts?'

—Matthew 9:4, NIV

CENTER YOUR LIFE ON JESUS

WHY DO YOU ENTERTAIN EVIL THOUGHTS (?)

Jesus had just crossed the line—and religious dignitaries keeping an eye on Jesus caught him in the act.

This flashy new rabbi had just done the unthinkable.

Right out loud—in front of God and everyone sardined in and around the house where Jesus stood—Jesus had dared to *forgive a man's sins*.

Something only God himself had the authority to do.

The rabbis in the back of the room exchanged startled glances; then their eyes hardened. Inching forward, they strained to catch every word Jesus said, words they'd throw in his face later when they demanded he be stoned to death as a blasphemer.

And then—the spotlight shifted.

Jesus pointed at them. Heads swiveled in their direction as Jesus called out, "Why do you entertain evil thoughts in your hearts?"

Evil *thoughts*? Could this guy read their *minds*?

What was an uncomfortable revelation for these accusers may be equally uncomfortable for us: Jesus is as concerned about what's happening inside us as he is about what we do.

A good deed done for the wrong reason? We may fool everyone else, but we aren't fooling Jesus. Hatred we hide from everyone but ourselves? He sees it.

To be so well known and completely understood by Jesus…how does that strike you?

Is it a comfort? Or a concern?

Or both?

WHY DO YOU ENTERTAIN EVIL THOUGHTS ?

AS YOU SPOKE WITH JESUS, WHAT DID YOU DISCOVER ABOUT HIM?

AS JESUS SPOKE WITH YOU, WHAT DID HE HELP YOU DISCOVER ABOUT YOURSELF?

Two blind men were sitting beside the road. When they heard that Jesus was coming that way, they began shouting, 'Lord, Son of David, have mercy on us!'

'Be quiet!' the crowd yelled at them.

But they only shouted louder, 'Lord, Son of David, have mercy on us!'

When Jesus heard them, he stopped and called, 'What do you want me to do for you?'

—Matthew 20:30-32, NLT

WHAT DO YOU WANT ME TO DO FOR YOU ?

The dusty road from Jericho to Jerusalem slanted ever upward, a steady, demanding, uphill trek for Jesus and his disciples.

And they weren't making the trek alone—far from it. A crowd shuffled along after them, anxious to cover the 18 miles, enter Jerusalem, and relax into whatever comforts awaited them.

And then they came upon two blind men sitting next to the road. Two blind men who wouldn't shut up.

The men shouted for Jesus to have mercy on them. When told to quiet down, they yelled even louder, desperate for Jesus to hear them.

He did.

And to the dismay of the crowd, everything halted as Jesus paused to call out to the blind men, "What do you want me to do for you?"

It seemed an odd question.

The men were obviously blind. What else could they want but their sight? Vision would unlock them from poverty. From their narrow world. From social stigma.

Yet Jesus asked…and waited for their answer.

It's a question Jesus still asks people who call out to him… people like us.

He asks, and he pauses, and he gives us time to consider our response.

What do we *really* want Jesus to do for us?

Imagine he's heard your shout for help and has asked what you *really* want, what you *really* need.

How will you answer?

WHAT DO YOU WANT ME TO DO FOR YOU ?

AS YOU SPOKE WITH JESUS, WHAT DID YOU DISCOVER ABOUT HIM?

AS JESUS SPOKE WITH YOU, WHAT DID HE HELP YOU DISCOVER ABOUT YOURSELF?

"What do you think? There was a man who had two sons. He went to the first and said, 'Son, go and work today in the vineyard.'"

—Matthew 21:28, NIV

CENTER YOUR LIFE ON JESUS

Jesus was teaching in the Temple when a posse of chief priests and elders interrupted, demanding to know what gave Jesus the right to do what he'd done.

The day before, Jesus had stormed through the courtyard, flipping over moneychangers' tables and sending coins cascading across the cobblestones. Tables toppled, chairs were tossed aside, people scrambled for safety or loose change…it was chaos.

Jesus' response was classic Jesus.

He engaged his accusers with a question, and then—before launching into a series of pointed parables—he asked, "What do you think?"

He offered to hear what they had to say about the truth he was sharing. To consider honest questions.

He welcomed their thoughts… and he welcomes yours.

And that's a good thing, because some of what Jesus taught—and teaches still—is baffling.

Turn the other cheek…even after abuse? Forgive seventy times seven…but isn't that enabling? The meek will inherit the earth… starting when?

What are your thoughts about this kingdom Jesus describes? your questions?

Tell Jesus—right now—and listen for his response.

AS YOU SPOKE WITH JESUS, WHAT DID YOU DISCOVER ABOUT HIM?

CENTER YOUR LIFE ON JESUS

AS JESUS SPOKE WITH YOU, WHAT DID HE HELP YOU DISCOVER ABOUT YOURSELF?

Jesus replied, 'Why were you looking for me? Didn't you know that it was necessary for me to be in my Father's house?'

—Luke 2:49, CEB

CENTER YOUR LIFE ON JESUS

WHY WERE YOU LOOKING FOR ME (?)

It's every parent's nightmare.

Your child vanishes into a crowd. In your frantic, gut-rending panic you retrace his steps. You push away the possibilities: Kidnapping. Injury. Death.

Mary and Joseph lived that nightmare for three endless days, searching Jerusalem in a mad scramble until they at last found their boy, their lost boy, sitting in the Temple.

And glancing up from his perch on the Temple steps, Jesus greeted them with this: "Why were you looking for me?"

As in, where else would I be, Mom?

As in, do I hug you or beat you within an inch of your life, kid?

Scripture is silent as to exactly how Jesus' earthly parents responded (use your imagination), but Jesus' question is still worth considering.

"Why were you looking for me?"

Joseph and Mary had a clear answer: Jesus was their son. They *had* to find him.

But why are *you* searching for Jesus? Or, more likely, continuing to search for a deeper relationship with Jesus?

What do you hope to find?

WHY WERE YOU LOOKING FOR ME ❓

AS YOU SPOKE WITH JESUS, WHAT DID YOU DISCOVER ABOUT HIM?

CENTER YOUR LIFE ON JESUS

AS JESUS SPOKE WITH YOU, WHAT DID HE HELP YOU DISCOVER ABOUT YOURSELF?

Inside, the high priest began asking Jesus about his followers and what he had been teaching them.

Jesus replied, 'Everyone knows what I teach. I have preached regularly in the synagogues and the Temple, where the people gather. I have not spoken in secret.'

'Why are you asking me this question? Ask those who heard me. They know what I said.'

—John 18:20-21, NLT

WHY ARE YOU ASKING ME THIS QUESTION (?)

Jesus had been arrested, bound, and then shoved from the Mount of Olives to the home of Annas, the former Jewish high priest.

And there Annas circled Jesus slowly, doing his best to be intimidating.

But Jesus didn't cower. When asked about his teachings, Jesus calmly reminded Annas he'd spoken publicly—in the Temple, no less.

"So why are you asking me this question?" Jesus said—earning him a jaw-snapping slap from a nearby Temple guard.

Jesus wasn't being disrespectful—he was asking to be treated fairly.

Jesus knew the interrogation was illegal. No witnesses had been called, no charges leveled. And Jesus couldn't be forced to incriminate himself.

So why was Jesus standing in Annas' house being questioned?

Called out, Annas waved Jesus away. Let him be someone else's problem.

By the way, that fairness Jesus requested never arrived.

Not at his trials. Not when he was abandoned by his friends. Not when he died on a cross for others' sins.

And yet, his question raises one for us: Are we treating Jesus unfairly?

Perhaps by expecting him to be someone he's not. To deliver on promises he never made. By asking for love and loyalty we're slow to return.

If Jesus were standing in your house, how would you answer his question?

WHY ARE YOU ASKING ME THIS QUESTION (?)

AS YOU SPOKE WITH JESUS,
WHAT DID YOU DISCOVER ABOUT HIM?

AS JESUS SPOKE WITH YOU, WHAT DID HE HELP YOU DISCOVER ABOUT YOURSELF?

He replied to him, 'Who is my mother, and who are my brothers?'

Pointing to his disciples, he said, 'Here are my mother and my brothers. Whoever does the will of my Father in heaven is my brother and sister and mother.'

–Matthew 12:48-50, NIV

CENTER YOUR LIFE ON JESUS

WHO IS MY MOTHER, AND WHO ARE MY BROTHERS ?

When Jesus' public ministry started putting him in harm's way—drawing angry words from powerful rabbis and concern from Romans suspicious of large gatherings—his family came calling.

Maybe to take him home. Cool him off. Keep him safe.

Or maybe just because he hadn't swung by the homestead lately, and they were hungry for a visit.

Whatever their reasons for coming, they got an unusual reception.

Told his family was waiting outside, Jesus pointed to his disciples and proclaimed his *real* family were the people doing God's will.

What do you make of that? What do you do with a Jesus who didn't drop everything and warmly hug his mother and kin?

Because that's how Jesus is often portrayed: always smiling, ever affirming, never demanding. And that's not the Jesus we meet in this encounter.

This is a Jesus who drew a line in the sand. If you wanted to be family—you joined him in obeying God.

How do you feel about *that* Jesus? The one who expects something of you?

What will you do with him?

WHO IS MY MOTHER, AND WHO ARE MY BROTHERS ?

AS YOU SPOKE WITH JESUS, WHAT DID YOU DISCOVER ABOUT HIM?

AS JESUS SPOKE WITH YOU, WHAT DID HE HELP YOU DISCOVER ABOUT YOURSELF?

But Jesus answered by saying to them, 'You don't know what you are asking! Are you able to drink from the bitter cup of suffering I am about to drink?'

'Oh yes,' they replied, 'we are able!'

—Matthew 20:22, NLT

ARE YOU ABLE TO DRINK FROM THE BITTER CUP OF SUFFERING I AM ABOUT TO DRINK ?

Jesus knew what lay ahead of him.

The torn, bleeding flesh. The agonizing beatings. The ridicule, spit, and savagery.

And when James and John came looking for a promotion, they all-too-quickly bragged that whatever Jesus endured, they'd endure.

If only they'd known.

Eventually both James and John drank from their own cups of suffering, as those who follow Jesus often do.

Cups brimming with hard stuff, like loving the unlovely. Forgiving the unforgivable. Giving again, again, and yet again to the utterly ungrateful.

Can you drink the cup of suffering Jesus drained dry? Unlikely... but your own cup is in front of you.

What's in it? And have you asked Jesus for his help dealing with it?

ARE YOU ABLE TO DRINK FROM THE BITTER CUP OF SUFFERING I AM ABOUT TO DRINK ?

AS YOU SPOKE WITH JESUS, WHAT DID YOU DISCOVER ABOUT HIM?

_____

_____

_____

_____

_____

_____

_____

_____

_____

_____

CENTER YOUR LIFE ON JESUS

AS JESUS SPOKE WITH YOU, WHAT DID HE HELP YOU DISCOVER ABOUT YOURSELF?

He asked a third time, 'Simon son of John, do you love me?'

Peter was sad that Jesus asked him a third time, 'Do you love me?' He replied, 'Lord, you know everything; you know I love you.'

—John 21:17a, CEB

CENTER YOUR LIFE ON JESUS

Three times.

Three times Jesus turned to his disciple Peter, and asked if Peter loved him.

Not "Do you like me?" Or "Are you a supporter?" Or "How about subscribing to my blog?"

"Do you *love* me?"

That question sets the bar high. Leaves no room for ambiguity. Asks for an all-in response.

It was a question for Peter…and a question for you, too.

Imagine Jesus taking a step closer to you, lowering his voice so just the two of you can hear. And then picture him asking you the same question he asked Peter.

How would you answer?

DO YOU LOVE ME ?

AS YOU SPOKE WITH JESUS, WHAT DID YOU DISCOVER ABOUT HIM?

AS JESUS SPOKE WITH YOU, WHAT DID HE HELP YOU DISCOVER ABOUT YOURSELF?

But Jesus, knowing their evil intent, said, 'You hypocrites, why are you trying to trap me?'

—Matthew 22:18, NIV

WHY ARE YOU TRYING TO TRAP ME ?

You might not like the Pharisees, those self-righteous traditionalists, but you've got to hand it to them: They knew how to lay a trap.

Their delegation approached casually, full of flattery, but only to lull Jesus into self-destructing when answering a carefully crafted question.

Is it lawful to pay taxes to Caesar?

A "yes" from Jesus, and they'd accuse him of denying God's sovereignty over Israel, turning the Jewish people against him.

A "no," and they'd trumpet Jesus as an enemy of Rome—guaranteeing an arrest and crucifixion.

But Jesus refused to play along, challenging the question with a question of his own: "You hypocrites, why are you trying to trap me?"

Given a choice between two options, he boldly picked a third.

Because that's where the truth lay.

Now and then people other than Pharisees have tried to trap Jesus, to manipulate him.

If you love me, you'll cure Mom's cancer.

You said if two of us agreed on something you'd do it, so give me that job.

Margie has six grandkids, and I've got none; you like kids, right?

In what ways—if any—have you found yourself trying to trap Jesus, to manipulate him in some way?

And how has that worked out for you?

WHY ARE YOU TRYING TO TRAP ME (?)

AS YOU SPOKE WITH JESUS, WHAT DID YOU DISCOVER ABOUT HIM?

AS JESUS SPOKE WITH YOU, WHAT DID HE HELP YOU DISCOVER ABOUT YOURSELF?

At this, many of his disciples turned away and no longer accompanied him.

Jesus asked the Twelve, 'Do you also want to leave?'

—John 6:66-67, CEB

CENTER YOUR LIFE ON JESUS

DO YOU ALSO WANT TO LEAVE (?)

So long as Jesus wowed the crowds with miracles, his approval ratings soared.

But then he started talking about eating his flesh and drinking his blood. About being the true, living bread of heaven. About being sent by God.

That's when the head-scratching and grumbling began, at first quietly and then more loudly.

That's when the crowds thinned.

And that's when Jesus, turning to his twelve disciples, asked, "Do you also want to leave?"

Now that Jesus had gotten to the tough stuff, now that he'd declared who he was and what it would cost to follow him, would his dozen closest disciples stay… or go?

The decision was theirs.

And it's yours as well.

When it gets costly to follow Jesus, when friends' eyebrows rise at the changes they see in you, when telling the truth means taking responsibility for something you'd rather avoid… will you stay? Or go?

How do you answer Jesus' question…and why do you answer as you do?

DO YOU ALSO WANT TO LEAVE ?

AS YOU SPOKE WITH JESUS, WHAT DID YOU DISCOVER ABOUT HIM?

AS JESUS SPOKE WITH YOU, WHAT DID HE HELP YOU DISCOVER ABOUT YOURSELF?

_____

_____

_____

_____

_____

_____

_____

_____

_____

_____

_____

Jesus went into a house, and the blind men followed him. He said to them, 'Do you believe that I can do this?'

'Yes, Lord,' they answered.

—Matthew 9:28, GW

CENTER YOUR LIFE ON JESUS

DO YOU BELIEVE THAT I CAN DO THIS ❓

The men looking for Jesus were determined to find him. No matter what. No matter who got in their way.

Unfortunately, they were blind—and blind in a world that did nothing to accommodate the sightless.

And they had no idea where Jesus was.

All they knew was that, earlier in the day, a hemorrhaging woman had been healed when she'd simply touched Jesus' robe. And if Jesus could do that, he most certainly could give them sight.

So they stumbled along behind a crowd they hoped was trailing Jesus. And when they'd at last found the house where Jesus was staying and, uninvited, barged inside, Jesus asked them this question: "Do you believe I'm able to do this?"

Of *course* they believed. That's why they'd *come*.

Except there's a world of difference between desperation and faith. Between belief and wishful thinking. Between *hoping* Jesus is all he says he is…and *knowing*.

As a Jesus-follower, you've got a lot riding on Jesus being able to deliver on his promises to forgive your sins…give you new life… give you *eternal* life.

So how would you answer Jesus' question?

Do you really believe he can do this?

Do you hope…or do you *know*?

DO YOU BELIEVE THAT I CAN DO THIS ❓

AS YOU SPOKE WITH JESUS, WHAT DID YOU DISCOVER ABOUT HIM?

AS JESUS SPOKE WITH YOU, WHAT DID HE HELP YOU DISCOVER ABOUT YOURSELF?

> And why do you worry about clothes? Notice how the lilies in the field grow. They don't wear themselves out with work, and they don't spin cloth.

—Matthew 6:28, CEB

CENTER YOUR LIFE ON JESUS

WHY DO YOU WORRY ABOUT CLOTHES (?)

When Jesus asked the crowd gathered on a hillside why they worried about their clothing, it was in a larger context.

He'd already asked why they worried about food, and why they treasured things that could rust or decay.

Clothing was just one more example of Stuff God Knows You Need So Don't Worry About It.

It was a novel concept then, and it's an equally novel one now.

Nowhere did Jesus suggest lying back and relaxing, assuming God will care for you with no effort on your part. But worrying endlessly about having enough?

Misplaced energy.

Perhaps your worries don't include clothing. You're set in the winter coat department. You're more concerned about your career. Your kids. Repaying your student debt.

Whatever it is that pegs your worry meter, fill it in below:

"Why do you worry about ___?"

Now picture Jesus posing that question to the crowd around him, sneaking a wink in your direction as he says it.

How would you answer his question?

WHY DO YOU WORRY ABOUT CLOTHES (?)

AS YOU SPOKE WITH JESUS, WHAT DID YOU DISCOVER ABOUT HIM?

AS JESUS SPOKE WITH YOU, WHAT DID HE HELP YOU DISCOVER ABOUT YOURSELF?

_____

_____

_____

_____

_____

_____

_____

_____

_____

_____

_____

> When he went back to the disciples, he found them asleep. He said to Peter, 'Couldn't you stay awake with me for one hour?'

—Matthew 26:40, GW

CENTER YOUR LIFE ON JESUS

COULDN'T YOU STAY AWAKE WITH ME FOR ONE HOUR (?)

Jesus' disciples felt as if they'd been on their feet for days.

There'd been the strain of clearing Jesus' path into Jerusalem, holding back crowds begging for a miracle. Staying on high alert for an attack from the Romans or Temple guards. Preparing, serving, and celebrating the Passover meal.

And there was Jesus himself—oddly distracted and subdued, as if he was gathering his strength for some coming disaster.

And then Jesus insisted on hiking to the Mount of Olives for prayer.

No wonder they couldn't keep their eyes open, even when Jesus asked them to. Even when they'd promised.

It simply was beyond them—their strength didn't stretch that far.

Which is why Peter found himself shaken awake by Jesus' question: "Couldn't you stay awake with me for one hour?"

Perhaps you've been in that spot: Your spirit was willing, but your flesh was weak.

Perhaps you're there now.

There's something to do or a temptation to overcome, but you just can't do it.

Rather than read Jesus' question as criticism, try reading it simply as a question: *Can't you do this?*

Well, no…we can't. Not without your help, Jesus.

Consider what's stressing you out, why you're feeling overwhelmed, and ask Jesus for his help.

COULDN'T YOU STAY AWAKE WITH ME FOR ONE HOUR (?)

AS YOU SPOKE WITH JESUS, WHAT DID YOU DISCOVER ABOUT HIM?

_____

_____

_____

_____

_____

_____

_____

_____

_____

_____

AS JESUS SPOKE WITH YOU, WHAT DID HE HELP YOU DISCOVER ABOUT YOURSELF?

'What is your name?' Jesus asked, and the demon replied, 'Legion, for there are many of us here within this man.'

—Mark 5:9, TLB

CENTER YOUR LIFE ON JESUS

WHAT IS YOUR NAME ?

Early one morning, Jesus met a demon-possessed man on a narrow beach that traced the rugged eastern shoreline of the Sea of Galilee.

At first glance the encounter seems to include chitchat, a polite exchange of names.

But that's not the case.

In Jesus' day, a cultural belief held that to know someone's name was to have power over that person. Names mattered. They told a story.

Demons terrorizing the wild-eyed man knew Jesus' name, and story, and told them both when they called him, "Jesus, Son of the Most High God."

And when Jesus commanded the demons to speak their names, they obeyed—sort of. "Legion," they shrieked, "because there are many of us."

Since that day on the shore, Jesus' name—and story—haven't changed. What was true then is true today. He's still Jesus, still the Son of the Most High God.

But what about *your* name? Your story?

How would you answer if Jesus were to ask you, "What is *your* name?"

Tell him your name and what story you want it to tell others—and him.

Then ask him how he would describe you.

WHAT IS YOUR NAME ?

AS YOU SPOKE WITH JESUS, WHAT DID YOU DISCOVER ABOUT HIM?

AS JESUS SPOKE WITH YOU, WHAT DID HE HELP YOU DISCOVER ABOUT YOURSELF?

_____

_____

_____

_____

_____

_____

_____

_____

_____

_____

_____

> "For who is greater, the one who is at the table or the one who serves? Is it not the one who is at the table? But I am among you as one who serves.

—Luke 22:27, NIV

CENTER YOUR LIFE ON JESUS

FOR WHO IS GREATER, THE ONE WHO IS AT THE TABLE OR THE ONE WHO SERVES

Three years.

That's how long Jesus modeled servanthood for his dozen closest followers. Talked about it. Encouraged it. Pointed it out.

Yet even now, hours before he's arrested and tortured, Jesus has to step in to settle a squabble about who's greatest.

A squabble among men who weren't likely—*any* of them—to go home the grand prize winner of the local Mr. Greatest competition.

But Jesus doesn't blast them. Instead, he asks a question: Who is greater, the one who sits at the table, or the one who serves?

Like us, they probably knew the right answer.

They just didn't believe it… not really.

And, perhaps, we don't, either.

Not really.

We quickly slip into feeling entitled, expecting others to take care of tasks we're too busy or important to handle, to defer to our wishes, to anticipate and meet our needs.

And while that spot is fun, it's not where you're likely to run into Jesus.

Now, as during his time on earth, he's generally hanging out in the servants' hall rather than the grand ballroom. Unless he trudged up there to serve others.

How would you answer Jesus' question?

FOR WHO IS GREATER, THE ONE WHO IS AT THE TABLE OR THE ONE WHO SERVES ?

AS YOU SPOKE WITH JESUS, WHAT DID YOU DISCOVER ABOUT HIM?

_____

_____

_____

_____

_____

_____

_____

_____

_____

_____

AS JESUS SPOKE WITH YOU, WHAT DID HE HELP YOU DISCOVER ABOUT YOURSELF?

_____

_____

_____

_____

_____

_____

_____

_____

_____

_____

_____

_____

> And what do you benefit if you gain the whole world but lose your own soul?

—Matthew 16:26a, NLT

CENTER YOUR LIFE ON JESUS

WHAT DO YOU BENEFIT IF YOU GAIN THE WHOLE WORLD BUT LOSE YOUR OWN SOUL ?

Sometimes when Jesus asked questions, he wasn't looking for answers.

He was making a point—and this is one of those times.

Jesus had started preparing his disciples for what was coming. He told them they'd be going to Jerusalem where Jesus would suffer, die, and rise again.

Peter pulled Jesus aside for a private conversation. Not to worry, Peter said, it wasn't going to happen. No way, no how.

Perhaps, puffing out his chest, Peter reassured Jesus he wouldn't *let* it happen.

Jesus' response was pointed and memorable.

He *would* face what was waiting for him in Jerusalem. And it was time for the disciples to set aside their own agendas and get in line to follow him.

That's where they'd find life. *That's* where their souls would be safe.

The question Jesus asked— "What do you benefit if you gain the whole world but lose your own soul?"—got the disciples' attention.

Because nothing is worth losing your soul. Nothing.

What was true in Jesus' day is true now: The place to find life… the place your soul is safe…is when you're following Jesus.

The disciples forgot that.

And, occasionally, so do we.

Ask Jesus where—if anywhere— you might better fall in line behind him.

And listen for his answer.

WHAT DO YOU BENEFIT IF YOU GAIN THE WHOLE WORLD BUT LOSE YOUR OWN SOUL ?

AS YOU SPOKE WITH JESUS, WHAT DID YOU DISCOVER ABOUT HIM?

CENTER YOUR LIFE ON JESUS

AS JESUS SPOKE WITH YOU, WHAT DID HE HELP YOU DISCOVER ABOUT YOURSELF?

> What would you do if you had a hundred sheep and one of them wandered off? Wouldn't you leave the ninety-nine on the hillside and go look for the one that had wandered away?

—Matthew 18:12, CEV

CENTER YOUR LIFE ON JESUS

Jesus put a question to his audience.

A man has a hundred sheep, and one wanders off. Won't he leave ninety-nine grazing up in the hills to track down the one who disappeared?

Any sensible shepherd listening would have answered, "Maybe."

Because it all depends.

Will setting out to find the wanderer put the rest of the flock at risk?

Does the lost sheep cause more trouble than she's worth?

Is this the first time it's happened, or the fifty-first?

Fortunately, God's not a sensible shepherd. He's one who loves. Who cares not just for his flock; but the individuals in it—even those who sometimes wander away.

Picture the "lost sheep" in your life.

Friends or family who've somehow strayed. Who are high maintenance. Who occasionally feel like more trouble than they're worth.

How willing are you to let God reach out to them through you? To reflect his patience, his grace, his invitation to discover joy in him?

Jesus described what sort of shepherd God is.

Ask Jesus what sort of shepherd you're turning out to be.

WOULDN'T YOU LEAVE THE NINETY-NINE ON THE HILLSIDE AND GO LOOK FOR THE ONE THAT HAD WANDERED AWAY (?)

AS YOU SPOKE WITH JESUS, WHAT DID YOU DISCOVER ABOUT HIM?

CENTER YOUR LIFE ON JESUS

AS JESUS SPOKE WITH YOU, WHAT DID HE HELP YOU DISCOVER ABOUT YOURSELF?

> About the ninth hour Jesus cried out with a loud voice, saying, 'Eli, Eli, lama sabachthani?' that is, My God, My God, why have You forsaken me?

—Matthew 27:46, NASB

CENTER YOUR LIFE ON JESUS

MY GOD, MY GOD, WHY HAVE YOU FORSAKEN ME (?)

He didn't call God "Father."

Jesus *always* addressed God as "Father," reflecting their intimacy. A reminder of their loving, soul-satisfying relationship.

But not this time.

Not as Jesus bled out on a cross, his face raised to a roiling, darkening sky.

Quoting Psalm 22, Jesus choked out an agonized appeal:

"Why have you forsaken me?"

He already knew the answer, of course. When he'd chosen to carry the full weight and fury of sin, he knew this was the price.

But while Jesus knew his answer, you might not know yours.

Not when pain, anger, or disappointment has prompted you to cry out, *"God, where are you?"* *"God, why don't you do something?"*

If those words feel familiar, if you've heard yourself saying something like them somewhere along your journey, say them again now.

Ask God, and listen for his answer.

MY GOD, MY GOD, WHY HAVE YOU FORSAKEN ME ?

AS YOU SPOKE WITH JESUS,
WHAT DID YOU DISCOVER ABOUT HIM?

AS JESUS SPOKE WITH YOU, WHAT DID HE HELP YOU DISCOVER ABOUT YOURSELF?

_____

_____

_____

_____

_____

_____

_____

_____

_____

_____

When they arrived, Jesus saw that all was in great confusion, with unrestrained weeping and wailing.

He went inside and spoke to the people.

'Why all this weeping and commotion?' he asked. 'The child isn't dead; she is only asleep!'

—Mark 5:38-39, TLB

CENTER YOUR LIFE ON JESUS

WHY ALL THIS WEEPING AND COMMOTION ?

Poor Jairus.

After frantically tracking down Jesus, falling at his feet, begging Jesus to come heal his dying daughter, and then hurrying Jesus toward his home, everything fell apart.

Jesus suddenly stopped in the street, asking the crowd swarming around him who had reached out and touched his clothes.

Touched his clothes? Jairus' daughter was nearby, gasping for breath. Every second counted. And Jesus was worried about who'd *touched* his clothes?

And then, the unthinkable. Friends found Jairus and broke the news.

He was too late. His daughter was dead. It was over.

Except…it wasn't.

From a fog of grief Jairus heard Jesus tell him not to fear, to trust him. Then, together, they came to the house where Jairus' daughter lay, pale and motionless.

Jesus' question, coming through the door, must have startled the mourners: "Why all this commotion and weeping?"

But Jesus knew something they didn't: Now that he'd arrived, so had life. Wherever Jesus is, there's no need for wailing and commotion.

Not that it always feels that way.

If Jesus were to walk through your door and ask why the commotion in your life, why the wailing, what would you say?

What keeps you from being unafraid? From believing?

WHY ALL THIS WEEPING AND COMMOTION ?

AS YOU SPOKE WITH JESUS,
WHAT DID YOU DISCOVER ABOUT HIM?

AS JESUS SPOKE WITH YOU, WHAT DID HE HELP YOU DISCOVER ABOUT YOURSELF?

> "If you love those who love you, do you deserve a reward? Even the tax collectors do that!"

—Matthew 5:46, GW

IF YOU LOVE THOSE WHO LOVE YOU, DO YOU DESERVE A REWARD ❓

Jesus' followers knew the Mosaic law commanded them to love their neighbors. They'd heard it preached in the synagogue for years.

And most of them had also heard the unofficial corollary some teachers of the day tacked on: "Unless those neighbors aren't Jewish."

Jesus didn't buy it.

Love wasn't just for the people who were like you. Who agreed with you. Who believed what you believed.

Jesus' idea of "neighbor" was far broader than many other rabbis' definition of the word. He must have raised a few eyebrows when he told a crowd, "If you love those who love you, do you deserve a reward? Even the tax collectors do that!"

Jesus didn't wait for their answer because the answer was clear: If you follow him, you'll love as he loves. And you'll love the people he chooses to love which is… everyone.

Even people who don't especially like you.

Suppose Jesus asked that question again, this time pausing for an answer. Your answer.

"If you love those who love you, do you deserve a reward?"

What would you say…and why?

IF YOU LOVE THOSE WHO LOVE YOU, DO YOU DESERVE A REWARD (?)

AS YOU SPOKE WITH JESUS, WHAT DID YOU DISCOVER ABOUT HIM?

CENTER YOUR LIFE ON JESUS

AS JESUS SPOKE WITH YOU, WHAT DID HE HELP YOU DISCOVER ABOUT YOURSELF?

> "Why do you call me 'Lord, Lord' and don't do what I say?

—Luke 6:46, CEB

WHY DO YOU CALL ME 'LORD, LORD' AND
DON'T DO WHAT I SAY (?)

Jesus had prayed through the night and then, come daybreak, made his way down a mountainside where a crowd waited for him.

He healed the sick, confronted unclean spirits, and taught anyone who'd listen.

And Jesus asked a question that likely caught more than a few in the crowd off guard: "Why do you call me 'Lord, Lord,' and don't do what I say?"

Ouch.

Jesus was stating the obvious: He had a huge fan club, but far too few followers. Far too few people who not only listened, but lived out his teachings.

It's easy to see how Jesus' words might have stung. Might have angered some who heard them…and prompted others to feel guilty.

His question still packs a punch—and it's been 2,000 years since he asked it.

And it still can leave those who hear it—like us—uncomfortable.

Jesus wasn't asking for perfection from his followers. He knew not to expect that from them—or us.

But he did ask for commitment and obedience.

When you consider Jesus' question, what emotion rises up in you?

And why do you feel as you do?

WHY DO YOU CALL ME 'LORD, LORD' AND DON'T DO WHAT I SAY ?

AS YOU SPOKE WITH JESUS, WHAT DID YOU DISCOVER ABOUT HIM?

_____

_____

_____

_____

_____

_____

_____

_____

_____

AS JESUS SPOKE WITH YOU, WHAT DID HE HELP YOU DISCOVER ABOUT YOURSELF?

> Do you think I have come
> to bring peace to the earth?
> No, I have come to divide people
> against each other!

—Luke 12:51, NLT

DO YOU THINK I HAVE COME TO BRING PEACE TO THE EARTH ❓

For someone described as the Prince of Peace, Jesus had disturbing news for his followers: Walking in his footsteps leads to conflict.

Including conflict within families.

Though speaking in front of a crowd that numbered in the thousands, Jesus pulled no punches.

After asking, *"Do you think I came to bring peace?"* he answered his own question by warning that his teachings were hard. That sacrifice was involved. And it was wise to prepare for rough waters ahead.

All of which makes sense.

Living out kingdom values in a non-kingdom world puts you at odds with culture… institutions…even friends and family. At times people around you will scratch their heads, wondering what you're doing, who you've become.

But still…how do you answer Jesus' question?

Do you expect him to bring peace to your life…or conflict… or both?

Tell Jesus your answer to his question—and why you answer as you do.

DO YOU THINK I HAVE COME TO BRING PEACE TO THE EARTH (?)

AS YOU SPOKE WITH JESUS,
WHAT DID YOU DISCOVER ABOUT HIM?

AS JESUS SPOKE WITH YOU, WHAT DID HE
HELP YOU DISCOVER ABOUT YOURSELF?

Jesus saw him lying there, and he knew that the man had been sick for such a long time; so he asked him, 'Do you want to get well?'

—John 5:6, GNT

CENTER YOUR LIFE ON JESUS

DO YOU WANT TO GET WELL ❓

While Jesus was in Jerusalem for a feast day, he passed by the pool of Bethesda.

Lying beneath five covered porches were dozens of the sick and maimed, each hoping the stories they'd heard were true: When the water rippled, whoever got into the pool first would be healed.

Jesus carefully picked his way among the sick and injured until he stood next to the well-worn mat of a man who'd hoped for healing for 38 years—with no results.

Jesus leaned down and asked, "Would you like to get well?"

Interesting question… because getting well came with consequences.

If the man was supporting himself as a beggar, that ended the moment he became able-bodied.

His longstanding friendships at the pool would end.

And his future? That would take work, no question about it.

So Jesus respectfully asked permission to change this man's life. And he's equally respectful today when it comes to changing other lives… yours included.

Consider Jesus' question for a moment.

In what ways—if any—do you want to be well?

And does Jesus have your permission to help that happen?

AS YOU SPOKE WITH JESUS, WHAT DID YOU DISCOVER ABOUT HIM?

AS JESUS SPOKE WITH YOU, WHAT DID HE HELP YOU DISCOVER ABOUT YOURSELF?

And the Jewish leaders slipped away one by one, beginning with the eldest, until only Jesus was left in front of the crowd with the woman.

Then Jesus stood up again and said to her, 'Where are your accusers? Didn't even one of them condemn you?'

—John 8:9-10, TLB

Humiliated. Shamed. Dragged before a condemning crowd, shoved facedown on the paving stones of the Temple courtyard.

This woman heard the bickering voices overhead, these men demanding to know what the teacher had to say about her sentence for adultery. Should they stone her? The law of Moses gave them the right.

Jesus knelt; she could see him through the curtain of her hair.

Once, then twice, he stooped to write in the dust, ignoring the harsh voices.

Then, one by one, the voices silenced. Her accusers drifted away into the crowd.

At last Jesus invited her to look around. Was there no one to accuse her?

Her voice quavering, she answered, "No, sir."

The powerful men who'd bruised and bullied her were gone. Only Jesus was left…and he forgave her.

That's the Jesus who loves you. When other voices condemn you, remind you of your past, point out your shortcomings, his is the steady, kind voice that brings you life. That speaks forgiveness.

Even if there is someone accusing you—even if it's your own voice that accuses you most loudly—those voices can't drown out the voice that matters most.

What is that voice—the voice of Jesus—saying to you now?

AS YOU SPOKE WITH JESUS, WHAT DID YOU DISCOVER ABOUT HIM?

AS JESUS SPOKE WITH YOU, WHAT DID HE HELP YOU DISCOVER ABOUT YOURSELF?

Jesus took the blind man's hand and led him out of the village. He spit into the man's eyes and placed his hands on him. Jesus asked him, 'Can you see anything?'

—Mark 8:23, GW

Spit? Really? *Medicinal* spit?

Some scholars suggest that Jesus spit on a blind man's eyes for a very practical reason: to lubricate and separate eyelids that had long-ago crusted together.

The blind man who'd asked for healing didn't object, so Jesus granted his plea for sight—gradually.

At first, partial sight was restored. Then, full vision.

But during the process Jesus asked this question: "Do you see anything?"

The answer was "yes," but the blind man wanted more. He wasn't content seeing vague shapes moving around—he wanted to see clearly. He wanted more.

And Jesus provided it.

Consider the state of your vision. Not your ability to read these words, but your ability to see Jesus clearly.

With that in mind, how would you answer Jesus' question? Do you see anything? Do you see a vague shape moving in the shadows, or something more?

And if you want more, how might Jesus respond?

Ask Jesus what would help you see him more clearly. He'll know the answer.

AS YOU SPOKE WITH JESUS,
WHAT DID YOU DISCOVER ABOUT HIM?

_____

_____

_____

_____

_____

_____

_____

_____

_____

_____

AS JESUS SPOKE WITH YOU, WHAT DID HE HELP YOU DISCOVER ABOUT YOURSELF?

> "Jesus knew that the disciples were grumbling about this and he said to them, 'Does this offend you?'"

—John 6:61, CEB

DOES THIS OFFEND YOU ❓

Jesus' disciples were muttering to one another about Jesus' teaching.

Tracking with him was getting hard…maybe too hard.

It wasn't that they failed to understand what Jesus was saying. It was that they *did* understand—they understood all too well.

That's what made it hard.

Jesus' teaching wasn't hard to understand…it was hard to accept.

Jesus expected so much from them; he called them to embrace such radical change. He was asking for—demanding, actually—more than most of those who trailed along after him were willing to give.

And when Jesus saw their discomfort, he didn't back down. Not an inch.

"Does this offend you?" he asked…but they could tell he didn't care.

Clearly, following Jesus—centering their lives on him—would require more from them than they'd anticipated.

And the same might be true for us.

How would drawing closer to Jesus—giving yourself fully to him—challenge and change you?

Ask Jesus to share his thoughts on the matter.

Just don't expect him to compromise.

AS YOU SPOKE WITH JESUS, WHAT DID YOU DISCOVER ABOUT HIM?

AS JESUS SPOKE WITH YOU, WHAT DID HE HELP YOU DISCOVER ABOUT YOURSELF?

'Why are you crying?' he asked her.
'Who are you looking for?'

She thought he was the gardener. 'Sir,' she said, 'if you have taken him away, tell me where you have put him, and I will go and get him.'

—John 20:15, TLB

CENTER YOUR LIFE ON JESUS

Mary Magdalene had come to find Jesus, but she didn't expect to meet him—not like this.

Not alive and standing in the very garden where Mary expected his body to be sealed in a tomb.

Not asking her, "Who is it you are looking for?"

Mary isn't the only one who's experienced the shock—and then the awe—of encountering Jesus in unlikely places. Because he's like that: He goes where he wants, when he wants.

But those who experience Jesus often have this in common: They're expectantly seeking him.

Mary was…and perhaps you are, too.

Or maybe you're more comfortable leaving Jesus where he's least intrusive: gazing down from stained glass windows or safely tucked away in study pages. Someplace he can't rattle your world or pull you into conversation.

If Jesus asked you who you were looking for and you mentioned his name, what might he say?

Give it a try. Tell him you're expecting to see him somehow working in your world. Invite him to be part of your week.

And then keep an eye open. He'll be by.

AS YOU SPOKE WITH JESUS, WHAT DID YOU DISCOVER ABOUT HIM?

AS JESUS SPOKE WITH YOU, WHAT DID HE HELP YOU DISCOVER ABOUT YOURSELF?

Then some Pharisees and experts in Moses' Teachings came from Jerusalem to Jesus. They asked, 'Why do your disciples break the traditions of our ancestors? They do not wash their hands before they eat.'

He answered them, 'Why do you break the commandment of God because of your traditions?'

—Matthew 15:1-3, GW

CENTER YOUR LIFE ON JESUS

WHY DO YOU BREAK THE COMMANDMENT OF GOD BECAUSE OF YOUR TRADITIONS (?)

When a delegation of religious legal scholars showed up to investigate Jesus, he made quite the impression.

Just not a very positive one.

Questioned about why Jesus' disciples didn't wash their hands before eating bread, Jesus cut to the chase.

The problem wasn't his disciples, he said. The problem was that these religious leaders valued their traditions (like ritual handwashing) as much—perhaps more—than they valued God's actual commandments.

Which meant tradition was not only getting confused with God's message, it was getting in the way…and Jesus couldn't let that stand.

He wasn't about to let people substitute adhering to traditions for an actual relationship with God. What counted wasn't keeping the rules—and the Pharisees piled those on—it was loving and being all-in for God.

But if Jesus thought one round of torpedoes fired at tradition would put it back in its place, he was mistaken.

It's alive and well. And sometimes even the best-intentioned faith traditions still muddy the waters, still get in the way of clearly, passionately following Jesus.

In what ways might tradition be placing obstacles between you and Jesus?

Ask him.

WHY DO YOU BREAK THE COMMANDMENT OF GOD BECAUSE OF YOUR TRADITIONS ?

AS YOU SPOKE WITH JESUS, WHAT DID YOU DISCOVER ABOUT HIM?

AS JESUS SPOKE WITH YOU, WHAT DID HE HELP YOU DISCOVER ABOUT YOURSELF?

> Don't you have eyes? Why can't you see? Don't you have ears? Why can't you hear? Don't you remember?

—Mark 8:18, CEB

CENTER YOUR LIFE ON JESUS

DON'T YOU REMEMBER

Now and again it would be nice if the Bible came with a soundtrack.

This is one of those times, because it certainly *seems* Jesus was frustrated with his disciples.

While sailing across the Sea of Galilee, it came to light that none of the disciples had remembered to bring food. A quick search turned up a single loaf of bread, and Jesus, never one to waste a teachable moment, warned them to be wary of "the yeast of the Pharisees and Herod."

Which launched an argument about whose fault it was that they didn't have dinner.

Sigh…

Jesus pointedly reminded his disciples that he'd fed thousands of people with a few loaves of bread. Clearly he could, if he wished, turn the boat into a bakery.

Didn't they remember what he'd done?

How could they forget so soon?

Because they were like us, that's why. Quick to panic. Fast to forget.

Jesus' question–*Don't you remember?*–could easily be asked of us as well.

What has Jesus done in your life you want to be certain to hold close, to keep top of mind? To never forget?

DON'T YOU REMEMBER ?

AS YOU SPOKE WITH JESUS,
WHAT DID YOU DISCOVER ABOUT HIM?

_____

_____

_____

_____

_____

_____

_____

_____

_____

_____

_____

AS JESUS SPOKE WITH YOU, WHAT DID HE
HELP YOU DISCOVER ABOUT YOURSELF?

The Pharisees came and began to question Jesus. To test him, they asked him for a sign from heaven.

"He sighed deeply and said, 'Why does this generation ask for a sign? Truly I tell you, no sign will be given to it.'

—Mark 8:11-12, NIV

WHY DOES THIS GENERATION ASK FOR A SIGN ?

The Pharisees who came to verbally spar with Jesus insisted on witnessing a miracle. And not just any everyday healing or water-into-wine sleight of hand. They demanded to see something *spectacular*.

Maybe along the lines of Elijah calling down fire from the sky—that would suffice.

Which must have been tempting for Jesus, considering they were standing right there. Out in the open. Easy targets.

But Jesus simply sighed, stunned by the arrogance and audacity of religious leaders who refused to look past their preconceptions and see him for who he was.

Jesus refused. His miracles weren't about showmanship.

And besides, if who he was and what he'd done already didn't convince the Pharisees, a bolt of lightning splitting open the earth at their feet wouldn't make a difference either.

Jesus' question—Why does this generation ask for a sign?—wasn't just for that generation. It's for us, too.

Because we can be just as keen to ask Jesus to do something remarkable to impress us, to earn our respect.

But if his life, death, and resurrection aren't enough, what will be? What else could he do to inspire your greater confidence...prompt you to trust him more?

Have that conversation with him. See what he has to say.

WHY DOES THIS GENERATION ASK FOR A SIGN ?

AS YOU SPOKE WITH JESUS, WHAT DID YOU DISCOVER ABOUT HIM?

AS JESUS SPOKE WITH YOU, WHAT DID HE HELP YOU DISCOVER ABOUT YOURSELF?

After Jesus had washed his disciples' feet and had put his outer garment back on, he sat down again. Then he said:

'Do you understand what I have done?'

—John 13:12, CEV

DO YOU UNDERSTAND WHAT I HAVE DONE (?)

Jesus was big on show and tell.

He'd just wrapped a towel around his waist and done what only servants did: wash the feet of his guests.

And these guests were his increasingly uncomfortable disciples, the very men who'd pledged to follow and serve him.

For the most part they'd served him well. Set aside their businesses and home lives to travel with him, trudging the long roads beside him, soaking up his teaching.

But somehow they'd missed the notion of serving one another. They'd been too busy competing for status in the group to give that much thought.

So Jesus showed them how servanthood looked and felt, and then, lest they misunderstand the lesson, he asked, "Do you understand what I have done?"

He'd humbled himself. Served wholeheartedly and without reservation.

Just as he's served us… served you.

Humbly. Without reservation.

What would you say if Jesus were to ask you the same question he posed to those twelve men in an upper room?

DO YOU UNDERSTAND WHAT I HAVE DONE ?

AS YOU SPOKE WITH JESUS, WHAT DID YOU DISCOVER ABOUT HIM?

AS JESUS SPOKE WITH YOU, WHAT DID HE HELP YOU DISCOVER ABOUT YOURSELF?

_____

_____

_____

_____

_____

_____

_____

_____

_____

_____

> Don't you know me, Philip, even after I have been among you such a long time? Anyone who has seen me has seen the Father. How can you say, 'Show us the Father'?

—John 14:9, NIV

CENTER YOUR LIFE ON JESUS

DON'T YOU KNOW ME ?

Like father, like son.

That old saying is never truer than when considering Jesus and his heavenly Father.

Yet, somehow, even Jesus' closest friends didn't quite catch it. After hundreds of hours at his side, countless casual conversations, and a ringside seat as Jesus restored lepers' withered limbs, cast out demons, and raised the dead, Philip didn't make the connection.

Somehow, after so long, Jesus could look at his friends and say, "Don't you know me, even after I have been among you such a long time?"

It's easy to be around Jesus and still not know him.

Especially easy for *us*.

One reason is because we often circle around Jesus, studying him as if he were an historical artifact. We dissect his words, master facts about his life, pride ourselves on having the trivia down cold.

And as we poke and prod at his life, we somehow miss that he's alive...alive and speaking to us.

So step back. Put down your study guide and class notes. And don't worry about what factoids might appear on the final.

Speak to Jesus...and let him speak to you.

It's time the two of you got better acquainted.

DON'T YOU KNOW ME (?)

AS YOU SPOKE WITH JESUS, WHAT DID YOU DISCOVER ABOUT HIM?

AS JESUS SPOKE WITH YOU, WHAT DID HE HELP YOU DISCOVER ABOUT YOURSELF?

> Can any of you convict me of committing a sin? If I'm telling the truth, why don't you believe me?

—John 8:46, GW

CENTER YOUR LIFE ON JESUS

IF I'M TELLING THE TRUTH, WHY DON'T YOU BELIEVE ME ❓

Not only did some people who heard Jesus not believe in him, they wanted him dead.

Their anger so clouded their vision that they rejected Jesus out of hand.

Not because he'd lied. Jesus didn't lie.

Not because he misrepresented God. That never happened.

Not because he'd sinned. Jesus asked his accusers to point to any law he'd broken or any sin he'd committed in his life, and his challenge went unanswered.

They rejected him because they didn't want to hear the truth he told.

So they simply quit listening and began gathering stones to drive him away—preferably into an early grave.

And other than continuing to taunt Jesus, they never answered his question: "If I'm telling the truth, why don't you believe me?"

Truth is hard to hear sometimes... especially truth about ourselves.

But harder still is living when—like these people intent on attacking Jesus—we refuse to hear it.

Ask Jesus: What truth do you have for me? Truth about you... and about me?

IF I'M TELLING THE TRUTH, WHY DON'T YOU BELIEVE ME ?

AS YOU SPOKE WITH JESUS, WHAT DID YOU DISCOVER ABOUT HIM?

AS JESUS SPOKE WITH YOU, WHAT DID HE HELP YOU DISCOVER ABOUT YOURSELF?

"Which is easier—to say, 'Your sins are forgiven,' or to say, 'Get up and walk'?

—Matthew 9:5, CEB

CENTER YOUR LIFE ON JESUS

WHICH IS EASIER—TO SAY, 'YOUR SINS ARE FORGIVEN,' OR TO SAY, 'GET UP AND WALK' ?

The preachers and teachers evaluating Jesus were still trying to decide: Was this brash young rabbi pure evil or just deluded?

Was he a blasphemer or just one more mentally unbalanced, would-be Messiah?

And the jury was still out.

They'd watched him claim to forgive a paralyzed man's sins, which only God could do. That was one checkmark in the "blasphemer" column, but an insane man might make the same claim.

And then Jesus pointed to them and asked, "Which is easier—to say, 'Your sins are forgiven,' or to say, 'Get up and walk'?"

And the paralytic got up and walked.

Which sealed the deal. Whether Jesus was evil, deluded, or both, he'd just proven himself to be something his accusers couldn't and wouldn't abide.

He'd proven he was dangerous.

And he still is.

Jesus—the real Jesus—is dangerous. He's unafraid, impolite, uncompromising, slicing through to the heart with blazing truth. He turns the world upside down.

And he's here. And he sees you. And he loves you.

What will you say to him?

WHICH IS EASIER—TO SAY, 'YOUR SINS ARE FORGIVEN,' OR TO SAY, 'GET UP AND WALK' ?

AS YOU SPOKE WITH JESUS,
WHAT DID YOU DISCOVER ABOUT HIM?

_____
_____
_____
_____
_____
_____
_____
_____
_____
_____
_____

CENTER YOUR LIFE ON JESUS

AS JESUS SPOKE WITH YOU, WHAT DID HE HELP YOU DISCOVER ABOUT YOURSELF?

My sheep listen to my voice. I know
them and they follow me. I give
them eternal life. They will never
die, and no one will snatch them
from my hand.

—John 10:27-28, CEB

CENTER YOUR LIFE ON JESUS

JESUS...WHAT ARE YOU SAYING TO ME ?

And then there's this last question...

It's one you won't find in the Bible because it's a question Jesus has for you—and only you.

A question that can speak to you like none other. That can change your life in unpredictable ways.

What is it?

That's between you and Jesus.

Do this: Tell Jesus you're listening. That you're ready to hear him. That you'll answer as honestly and openly as you can.

And then live expectantly—because he will nudge that question into your thinking. Today, tomorrow, when the time is right, you'll hear from him.

What's Jesus' question for you?

And where might your answer take you?

JESUS...WHAT ARE YOU SAYING TO ME ?

AS YOU SPOKE WITH JESUS, WHAT DID YOU DISCOVER ABOUT HIM?

AS JESUS SPOKE WITH YOU, WHAT DID HE HELP YOU DISCOVER ABOUT YOURSELF?

NOTES

CENTER YOUR LIFE ON JESUS

CENTER YOUR LIFE ON JESUS

NOTES

CENTER YOUR LIFE ON JESUS